Anthony the Ant!

Written by: Andrea Hassell

Illustrations by: Hanna Butzlaff

The Butterfly Series™

To order additional copies of this book, contact:
Xlibris
1-888-795-4274
www.Xlibris.com
Orders@Xlibris.com

Anthony, the Ant is dedicated to my three children and grandchild,
Teniko, TeAnn, Tenae and Tegan who inspire me.
A special thanks to Terry Hassell for
for the initial vision for this book.
I wish to, also, thank Cheryl Carter
for her coaching and mentorship.

Anthony, the ant, wants to join his friends under the cherry trees on the other side of the river. He realizes, however, that it will be a challenge to reach them.

He looks around and spots a bridge. He walks towards the bridge, but as he gets closer he is not sure that the bridge will be able to support him.

Anthony, also, remembers that he is afraid of the water.

Does Anthony have enough faith in himself to believe that he will get to the other side?

As he starts to cross the bridge, the wind starts blowing fiercely. However, he is focused on getting to his friends. Halfway across the bridge, Anthony is blown into the water.

Although he is afraid, he is determined to reach the other side. Suddenly, a leaf appears next to him so he climbs on it.

Just as the leaf starts to sink, along comes a log. Anthony, who is determined to get to the other side to join his friends, climbs on the log.

The log flows down the river and stops right in front of the cherry tree.

Anthony is so excited to see his friends that he jumps off the log and runs to meet them. He briefly looks back at the river and smiles to himself because he realizes that he made it.

Anthony had faith!

Anthony was focused!

Anthony followed through with his goal!

As a result, he now gets to eat cherries with

his friends.

Parent/Teacher Discussion Guide

It is necessary for children to have faith and to believe it is possible to obtain their goals. Life will bring challenges, disappointments and discouragement but they should never give up. They must learn to remain focus by studying hard for school, practicing their musical instruments or staying committed to training to a particular sport. We must impress upon them the fact that they can achieve as long as they follow-through with their goals. This book will encourage your children to learn responsibility and to foster conversation on these principles.

Questions for thought:

1. What was Anthony's goal?
2. What was Anthony's biggest fear?
3. How did Anthony overcome his fears?
4. What would have happened had Anthony not followed through with his goals?
5. What provisions did nature provide for Anthony to achieve his goal?
6. Why was Anthony so excited in the end?

Practical Application

1. What are your goals?
2. What are some of your fears?
3. How do you think you can overcome your fears?
4. What happens when you do not follow through with your goals?

Printed in the United States
By Bookmasters